Growing, Truly

Riley Brown

BookLeaf
Publishing

India | USA | UK

Presentation by *BookLeaf Publishing*

Web: www.bookleafpub.com

E-mail: info@bookleafpub.com

ISBN: 9789358737585

First edition 2023

for my past, current, and future selves

PREFACE

In this book lay eighteen poems written out of a desire to simply express. There is a clear view of growth; within these chronological poems, my perspective shifted and I began seeing clearer. It is a raw record of my thoughts, memories, previously unsaid feelings, and my hopes and dreams. It is part of my truth.

trying

i try desperately to feel better
all the time
i'm
trying
to heal

buying
  flowers
analyzing
  my issues
specifying
  my needs
un-identifying
  with the things
that were holding me

        hostage

i am trying
to heal
the trauma
that is
underlying
everything

coping

i realized recently that much of what i do
is coping
and i'm still learning how to

i found that my singing
is my coping
and it is the breathing
and the being
still
and when i look at my nails
i see that it is the picking, too

and when i feel the words pile up in me
it is the writing
that is the coping

i never saw this before
that there is a need to cope
but don't we all feel it?
the weight of being human
being alive
and dealing with things familiar?

isn't it heavy for anyone else?
everyone else?

we cope just to keep on
just so we can hold on
wait it out a little longer
until we feel better

until a smile returns
or a laugh affirms
that this is why we're here

and so even when we're coping
we must remember the smile is near
laughter will sound in our ears
and that here
is where we're meant to be

it's fall now

i thought my struggles would change
like the seasons:
faded colors,
falling snow,
but no.

many things have changed;
(it's fall now)
but i'm still dealing with the same shit

i've always only wanted to be seen

i wonder if we would be kinder
if we knew what other people have gone through
if we got to hear
or see
their pain

i got no tip from a table once
i grew upset
Asshole.
Piece of

shit.
was it me?
it was my energy
but maybe
if he'd seen
all the crying
he would have given me something

i don't think it was his money i wanted
but his understanding
of the wrong-doing
that's been done to me

every moment will pass

in the moments of bliss
(the laughter, mostly)
i cherish it

in the moments of sadness
(overthinking, really)
i think about getting past it

this, too, will pass
i think
but then i remember how
i must allow
--every--
moment to exist

With a Smile

You only have one life,
they said.
I know,
I said,
the same way I speak to my mother:
I get it, Mom.

But it is true
This moment will pass
And it will never come again
It is true
It is a blessing to be here
We are against all odds
and yet I'm going to live
upset?
bitter?
disappointed?
dissatisfied?
That time is over
Those moments have passed
Onto the next
with a smile

I Lied

There was a time
I
lied.
I tried
to find
myself,
and I did it through
buying things for my room
and wearing blue
hippie pants,
and I told myself
this is me
I am my brown hair
and my tendencies
I am an enemy
and my jealousies,
but this was never me.

Now I see
that the things that I was,
that I am,
are far greater than that.
I am my love
and my care
I am the air

I am the feeling of my feet bare
I am beauty
and I am a soul that is aware

Little Girl

The little girl in me is still playing Ghost in the
Graveyard
hiding behind the big rock
hoping to not be seen
or heard

The little girl in me is still standing around the
corner
waiting to shock someone
She anticipates the surprise
Hoping that when it occurs
it is not a negative one
but a positive

The Sun Shines

Grass under my palms
Great beam of light shining
on us, it will always be us

You lay on your stomach
just like when you sleep
You don't speak
but I do, just to say Bae,
I love you
or something like that

The sun shines on your hair
makes it look black
I love it
I run my fingers through it,
And as I sit with your head in my lap,
I feel wrapped
in Love
and Light

My sister's cat
comes along, tail up, curled
She meows
then turns around
I tell you to pet her

I her her she's a good girl
And I lay back down on the ground
knowing I'm surrounded
by Love,
and Light

Changing

This part of my life
feels different, better
The miserable me is no longer an ally

I must choose to smile, and laugh
I must believe I deserve it
For it is my destined path

I am no longer remaining stagnant
My power dormant
Resting between my drive and fragments of
pleasure

I am done releasing negativity
Instead, I am expressing my creativity

I must write and read
And plant the seeds
of my future

This is a time of growth
This is a time to approach life
in a new way

The Little Things

Life is about the little things
And yes, it is about the big things you do,
like graduate, and build a career
and that dream you pursue

But it is about washing your hands, too
It is about cutting grapes
and looking out the window
and all the little mistakes

It is about studying your love's face
And the deep breath you take
and every warm embrace
Because the truth is

The little things make up the most of life

So if tomorrow you died
and you didn't appreciate the little things,
like when your hair finally dries
and your favorite paring knife
then what were you here for?
were you here just to live and die?

Honest

I will be honest:
It is hard to stay away from you
Tonight, I walked into my room
where my jacket hangs on a hook
and I got scared; I thought someone was there
Immediately I thought about calling you
"You must come over"
But the truth is, I just want you to
and also, even if I get scared without you
I am fine.
I mustn't rely on you for my happiness
You think that seeing each other is something
that should happen less
But I disagree
So now here I am
listening to a Joe Pera soundtrack
alone with my thoughts
and the black hanging jacket

I will/I will not

I will not just live and die!
I will not just work and die!
I will do the work to live well!
And I will do the living to die happy

You must remember

When you have just finished sex
and the wet kisses have dried on your neck
Yes, it is okay that you still remind yourself that
you're not an object

It is a few months back and you have just
finished sex
Soon you cry, then shout, you are freaking out
and he doesn't know what it's all about
but you are loud and relentless and he tries to
calm you down
but you can't.
The memories keep flooding and he just keeps
hugging you
Finally, he gets through to you:
Breathe out and in, and out again
and when you are ready,
you can tell me everything that you're carrying

But it happens again
and again
and again
but each time it gets better
and now, it is prevented

You have come a long way
It's true! You feel the pain less!
You have made progress!

But next time, when he declines your offering
and you try to hide your eyes watering
you must remember that you already
experienced the end of your suffering

He did not reject you
Yes, he loves the view of you
Yes, you are the only one he will pursue

and when you think of all the times you
withdrew
Do not hold it against yourself
For you had healing to do

Where is the line?

Where is the line between staying the same
and improving everything?
How can I love myself fully
if I constantly think about all the things I could
be?

Still Admiring

It is bright outside but the blinds are closed
It's past eleven
and I know you won't wake up for a few more
hours
So I admire your beauty
and get out of bed

I sit at my desk
and look at you periodically
still admiring your beauty

Scared

I am ten years old laying in bed
Moonlight shines onto the floor in stripes

I am on the bottom bunk
My sister is on top
She shifts, the bed squeaks

I am ten years old laying in bed
hugging my teddy bear
But that is not enough;
I am still scared.

I ask my sister if I can join her in her bunk
She reluctantly agrees
So when I find the courage
I rush to the foot of the bed,
climb so fast
and nestle myself beside her legs

I decide that feeling her kick
in the middle of the night
is better than feeling scared

Almost Twenty

You are almost twenty
and you hope that in two years you will be in
Colorado
among the mountains and fresh air
It's so pretty there

You are almost twenty
and it's weird
You have done so much growing.
There was floating
and hoping
and coping
and joking
and you did so good.
You have done so good

You are almost twenty
and you have so much to do
Like travel and learn languages
and inspire people and write
You must play piano and learn jiu-jitsu
and make videos and be a light

You are almost twenty and your life is just
beginning

You can slow down and breathe and appreciate
and be
You can learn and you can love and you can feel
what it means to be free

You are almost twenty and there is so much
ahead of you
a career
and kids
and late night talks that are taboo
there are more hugs
and more love
and mismatched socks to get rid of
there is takeout food
and home cooked meals
and brushing your teeth and your hair
there are museums and art
and there is time to become smart

You are almost twenty
so enjoy it while it lasts
because soon you'll be fifty,
part of you wishing you could come back